The Mystery of UFOs

Chris Oxlade

Heinemann Library
Des Plaines, Illinois

Designed by AMR Ltd

Cover photograph reproduced with permission of Paul Villa, Fortean Picture Library.

Printed in Hong Kong

03 02 01 00 99
10 9 8 7 6 5 4 3 2 1

Library of Congress Cataloging-in-Publication Data
Oxlade, Chris.
  The mystery of UFOs / Chris Oxlade.
    p. cm. – (Can science solve?)
  Includes bibliographical references and index.
  Summary: Discusses the phenomenon of unidentified flying objects, including notable sightings throughout history and possible explanations for them.
  ISBN 1-57572-806-0 (library binding)
  1. Unidentified flying objects—Sightings and encounters Juvenile literature. [1. Unidentified flying objects.] I. Title.
II. Series.
TL789.2.O95 1999
001.942—dc21   98-54488
                                                    CIP
                                                    AC

Acknowledgements

The Publishers would like to thank the following for permission to reproduce photographs:

Aviation Picture Library, p.19; Mary Evans Picture Library, pp.13 (top), 24, 26; K. Aarsleff, p.17; G. Adamski, p. 10; C. Hart Jr., p. 9; Fortean Picture Library, pp. 6, 7; W. Akins, p. 28; B. Askew, p. 20; D. Stacy, p.13 (bottom); F. Taylor, p. 23; A. Vieira, p. 29; P. Villa, p. 4; Science Photo Library/NASA, p.15; D. Parker, p.18.

Every effort has been made to contact copyright holders of any material reproduced in this book. Any omissions will be rectified in subsequent printings if notice is given to the publisher.

Some words in this book are shown in bold, **like this.** You can find out what they mean by looking in the glossary.

Contents

Unsolved Mysteries

For centuries, people have been puzzled and fascinated by mysterious creatures, places, and events. They seek answers to seemingly unanswerable questions. Is there really a monster living in Loch Ness? Did the lost city of Atlantis ever exist? Are crop circles clever hoaxes or messages from alien beings? Are UFOs tricks of the light, or are they vehicles from outer space? These are some of the mysteries that even baffle scientists. Many scientists have spent their entire careers trying to solve these mysteries. But just how much can science tell us? Can it really explain the seemingly unexplainable? Are there some mysteries that science simply cannot solve? Read on, and make up your own mind.

This book tells you about the history of UFOs, presents eyewitness accounts of sightings, and looks at the different theories that attempt to explain them.

What is a UFO?

The letters *UFO* stand for "Unidentified Flying Object." Most people think that UFO is simply another way of saying "alien spaceship," but it is not. A UFO is any light or object in the sky that cannot be explained. Some UFOs can't be seen by the human eye. They are detected by **radar**. Radar, such as that used by air traffic controllers, locates objects in the sky and in space.

This photograph of a UFO was taken by Paul Villa, near Albuquerque, New Mexico.

4

Did you know that more than 90 per cent of reported UFOs become IFOs—Identified Flying Objects. After taking a closer look, it turns out that what was sighted can be explained. Some are identified as aircraft, planets, or weather balloons, for example. But this still leaves many UFOs unexplained. What are they? The best known theory is that UFOs are spacecraft belonging to lifeforms from planets outside our **galaxy.** Some people believe that aliens are trying to learn about Earth. Others believe all UFOs are naturally occurring objects in the atmosphere, such as clouds. Some say that UFOs are **hallucinations** or hoaxes.

Is there any truth to stories of alien **abductions** and the media hype surrounding UFOs? Are UFOs worth investigating? Can science solve the mystery?

Beginnings of a Mystery

The UFO **phenomenon** first became international news in the late 1940s. But there are many reports of strange objects in the sky dating back thousands of years. Some UFOlogists—people that study UFOs—think that the Star of Bethlehem was a UFO. Some say the star appeared when Jesus was born and it's placement in the sky marks the site of his birth.

Some UFOlogists believe this 8,000-year-old painting from the Sahara Desert is of an alien space traveller.

Early UFOs

One of the earliest UFO sightings was made in China in 1914 B.C. "Ten flying suns" caused panic among the people. In 216 B.C., Roman troops saw several "ships in the sky" over Italy. There are several reports from Japan: in A.D. 1180, there was a "glowing vessel" in the sky; in 1235, there were strange moving lights overhead; and for 4 days in 1749, thousands of people in Japan saw 3 huge flying objects.

UFO hotspots

There have been reports of UFOs from all over the world. But there tend to be more reports from some areas than others. Where are these UFO "hotspots"? Most hotspots tend to be in highly populated areas where people are interested in UFOs. More reports of UFOs would be expected from these places because more people are looking for them. Top hotspots include Mexico City, Mexico; Warminster, England; and Gulf Breeze, Florida.

In 1897, a farmer in the state of Kansas, saw a "huge, cigar-shaped object the length of a football field" land in one of his fields. Inside the craft's glass cabin were six of the "strangest beings ever seen." When the ship departed, it carried away a cow on the end of a rope.

During World War Two, pilots from both sides who flew over Europe occasionally saw small balls of light that seemed to follow their aircraft. The "foo fighters"—perhaps named after the French word feu, which means "fire"—have never been explained.

Did You See That?

Here are some of the most famous UFO sightings reported.

Kenneth Arnold, Mount Rainier, U.S., 1947

Kenneth Arnold was flying over a mountain range searching for the wreck of a military transport plane. He saw a flash of light. When he looked to see where the flash came from, he saw nine objects moving "like a saucer would if you skipped it across water." He estimated that they were longer than a sperm whale, about 66 feet (20 meters) across, and flying at more than 1,200 miles (2,000 kilometers) per hour, 3 times faster than any aircraft of the time. Arnold's is one of the most famous sightings. After hearing his description, newspeople began using the term "flying saucer." Within days of Arnold's story hitting the newstands, UFO reports began flooding in from all over the United States.

Kinds of close encounters

American UFOlogist Dr. J. Allen Hynek devised this classification system for encounters with UFOs and aliens:

- *CE1 (Close Encounter of the First Kind): When a UFO is spotted at a distance, such as a light or object in the sky.*
- *CE2: When a UFO leaves a sign of its presence, such as marks on the ground.*
- *CE3: When the eyewitness sees alien creatures inside or outside a UFO.*
- *CE4: When a person is abducted by aliens.*
- *CE5: When a person talks to or communicates with an alien.*

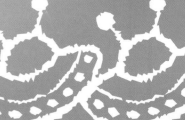

In 1951, hundreds of people in Lubbock, Texas, reported seeing formations of lights flying overhead. They said the lights made the shape of a wing. These lights were never explained.

UFO on film, New Zealand, 1978

An Australian TV reporter and a film crew were on a plane. They were looking for a UFO that had been reported a few days earlier. They saw and filmed several bright lights in the sky and an object with a bright base and dome. This domed craft appeared to be tracking the plane. **Radar** on the ground confirmed that an object was there. However, it was never identified.

The Trident sighting, Portugal, 1976

A British Airways Trident aircraft was flying south of Lisbon, Portugal. The crew heard air traffic control report that their radar detected a UFO. From their windows, the Trident's crew and passengers saw a bright light and a long cigar-shaped object. The object was moving toward the light. The crews of two other aircraft confirmed the sighting. An hour later, on the Trident's return flight, radar detected an object the size of a supertanker in the same place, but the crew saw nothing.

9

Meeting the Aliens

On these pages, you can read reports of CE4s and CE5s. These include meetings with aliens and **abductions** by aliens. For the most part, the people who claim to have been abducted can't remember what happened. However, all report that hours are missing from their lives and they have an unshakable feeling that something happened to them during that time.

George Adamski claims to have photographed many UFOs. He calls this one a "Venusian interplanetary carrier." He says this photo was taken through an astronomical telescope.

All in the mind?

*Many **psychologists** think that alien abductions are not real events. They say that people who believe they have been abducted may have experienced the event while in a dreamlike state. This dream state is called "sleep paralysis." It can happen just before falling into deep sleep. When in a state of sleep paralysis, the dreamer feels awake.*

George Adamski, California, 1952

This celebrated case is the first example of a human meeting an alien. Adamski claims that one afternoon he was watching and photographing a flying saucer when a humanlike alien approached him. Using hand gestures and telepathy, the alien told Adamski that he was from Venus. Two families witnessed the incident from a distance. This meeting was the first of many for Adamski. He claims to have been taken by a flying saucer to Mars, Saturn, and Jupiter. He also claims to have met inhabitants of each planet. However, Adamski has no proof of his encounters.

Betty and Barney Hill, New Hampshire, 1961

This was the first widely-reported case of people being abducted by aliens. The Hills were driving home late at night when they saw a bright light ahead. The light got brighter and closer. It appeared to be moving. They stopped the car and Barney got out. He saw an object hovering above the ground. As he approached it, he saw a dozen "people" inside. He ran back to the car and the couple drove off. Afterwards, they were in a "sedated" state for some time. Ten days later, Betty began to have nightmares. She dreamed that aliens took her and Barney into their spaceship and examined them. Betty was certain that she was remembering real events. Under hypnosis, both Betty and Barney recalled the abduction. Nothing can be proved.

It's Official

Today, the world's governments do not investigate UFO sitings reported by the general public. The military, however, does investigate UFOs if they are detected by their **radar.** In the past, all reports, regardless of the source, were studied. In the United States from the 1940s through the 1960s, the Air Force (USAF) was the military branch responsible for investigating UFOs. At that time, the **Cold War** was at its height. Some UFOs were thought to be newly developed Russian aircraft. Although it was impossible, the Air Force wanted to identify and have an explanation for all sightings.

Project Blue Book

Between 1952 and 1969, the USAF kept a record of all the UFO reports it received. This record was called Project Blue Book. In all, it listed 12,318 sightings. All were investigated and most were explained. But 701 sightings remain a mystery.

Men in black

Have you heard of the 1998 film Men in Black*? Do you know who the men in black really were? Like in the movie, they were men in dark suits and dark glasses. The Men in Black visited UFO eyewitnesses and investigators, warning them to keep quiet about their experiences. Some people say that the Men in Black were agents of the United States government. Others say they were aliens!*

The conspiracy theory

Many UFOlogists are convinced that the governments of the world have conclusive evidence that some UFOs are actually alien spacecraft. They claim that there is a cover-up headed by the U.S. CIA (Central Intelligence Agency) to prevent panic. In the United States, the Air Force formed the Condon Committee. The Condon Committee is a group of engineers and scientists that investigates UFOs. Although none of the UFOs they studied have turned out to be alien spacecraft, UFOlogists doubt their conclusions.

This debris was found in 1947 near Roswell Air Force Base, New Mexico. The USAF claims it is the remains of a weather balloon. Many UFOlogists say it is a flying saucer.

There are also reports that astronauts have encountered UFOs. One report claims that in 1969, Neil Armstrong saw a fleet of spacecraft on the moon during the Apollo 11 mission. **Conspiracy theorists** say that the astronauts were told to keep quiet. They believe that **NASA** faked the photographs of the moon landings.

Many strange lights have been seen in a military area in Nevada nicknamed "Area 51" by UFOlogists. The official story is that the area does not exist.

Are We Alone?

The case for UFOs being alien spacecraft would seem more believable if there was evidence that there is actually intelligent life in other parts of the universe. So how likely is it that other lifeforms exist, and how could we find out if it was there?

The chances of life

As of now, scientists think that the earth is the only planet in our **solar system** where there is life. The chances of intelligent life evolving on the earth must have been very small indeed, but it did.

Astronomers know that there are thousands of millions of stars like our sun in our **galaxy**. They know there are thousands of millions of galaxies in the universe. They have found evidence of large planets **orbiting** our neighboring stars. Therefore, it is not unreasonable to think that there may be other planets out there that can support life.

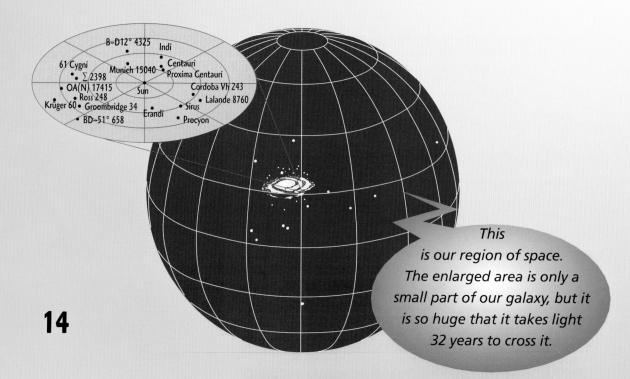

This is our region of space. The enlarged area is only a small part of our galaxy, but it is so huge that it takes light 32 years to cross it.

14

Signals from Earth

Trying to contact life on other planets has one huge problem—the distances involved. Radio signals travel at the speed of light,186,282 miles (300,000 kilometers) per second, but they still take more than four years to reach even our nearest star neighbor. And then one must wait for the reply to come back at the same speed. Many of the radio signals we use for communications on Earth are sent into space. The signals may be detected by other beings. In 1973, a simple **binary** radio message was sent to a cluster of stars called M13 in the hope that there is life on one of the many stars there. It will take 25,000 years to reach the cluster.

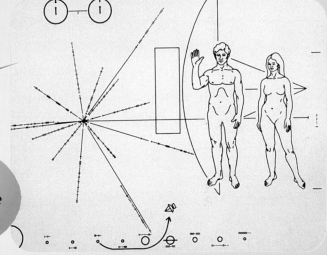

The plaque on the space probes Pioneer 10 *and* Pioneer 11 *would help intelligent forms of life find the earth if they ever found the probes.*

Listening out

In 1982, a group of Russian and American scientists set up a project known as SETI (Search for **Extraterrestrial** Intelligence). Scientists at SETI use a radio telescope to locate radio signals coming from outer space. So far, they have listened to thousands of stars. Although they have yet to find anything, there are millions more stars to tune into.

In 1977, American astronomer Bob Dixon detected a 37-second-long powerful radio signal. It came from a place in the **constellation** Sagittarius. The signal has never been repeated and may have been a random event.

Travel to the Stars

If one assumes that there is other intelligent life in the universe, could he or she ever visit it? More importantly for the explanation of UFOs, could that intelligent lifeform build a spacecraft and visit Earth?

The age of civilization

Astronomers think that our solar system was formed about 4,500 million years ago. The oldest **fossils** ever found are of simple sea-living organisms 3,000 million years old. Creatures began to inhabit land about 500 million years ago. Humanlike creatures evolved about 4 million years ago. Farming began about 10,000 years ago, and industry began about 300 years ago. Computers have been developed in the last 40 years. From this, you can see that the pace of technological change is speeding up. As we enter the 21st century, our knowledge of science is both vast and only the tip of the iceberg.

Gods or aliens?

There are theories that aliens visited the earth in ancient times. The theory states that aliens communicated with people and brought them technological advances. The evidence for this theory comes from archaeological finds called "out-of-place artifacts" (OOPARTS). These objects are thousands of years old but they have high tech components. One example is a 1,800-year-old ceramic pot found in Iraq. It acts as a battery. Another is a 5-1/2 inch (14 cm) long glider made in 200 B.C. It flies perfectly.

Now imagine a planet in another solar system a million years older than ours. What sort of scientific knowledge and technology might they have? Would they be advanced enough to build a spacecraft that could cross the vast expanse of space between our worlds? Currently, our spacecraft travel at about 24,000 miles (40,000 kilometers) per hour. That means it would take about 27,000 years to reach the nearest star, four light years away. But with a spacecraft capable of moving at one quarter the speed of light, about 150 million miles (250 kilometers) per hour, it would take about 16 years—much more practical!

These lines in Peru are claimed to be landing areas for UFOs that visited Earth thousands of years ago.

Identified Objects

Most of the UFOs reported by the public are actually normal objects or **optical illusions** created by the weather. On these pages you can find out which objects are often mistaken for UFOs.

Real flying objects

Aircraft are often reported as UFOs, especially at night when only their lights are visible. Helicopter lights confuse people because helicopters can hover in the air and move in any direction. Other flying objects that are often mistaken for UFOs are hot-air balloons, airships, weather balloons, kites, and birds. Weather balloons can be very confusing because they rise very high into the atmosphere. They are often silver and so they reflect the sunlight. These shapes are sometimes also distorted by **mirages.**

This is a type of weather balloon called a "meduse." Can you see why it might be reported as a flying saucer?

Some UFOs are seen on **radar** screens rather than with the naked eye. But radar can be fooled as well as people. Thick clouds, flocks of birds, and places where hot and cold air masses meet can produce misleading radar images.

In the United States, some reports of bizarre shapes in the sky have been explained as experimental aircraft, such as this Stealth fighter.

Space objects

Some of the UFOs reported are actually supposed to be in space. They may be natural or humanmade objects that astronomers know all about. Sometimes these objects are mistaken for UFOs because they reflect sunlight. For example, the planet Venus, the brightest planet in the sky, is often visible in the evening or morning. **Satellites** in low **orbits** around the earth look like tiny, fast-moving lights when the sun shines on them. Rockets taking off have also been mistaken for UFOs. Objects that hurtle through space and burn up as they enter the earth's atmosphere, such as **meteoroids** and parts of rockets, create streaks of light.

Weird Weather

It is thought that natural events in the earth's atmosphere can explain more than 90 per cent of the sightings of strange lights and shapes in the sky. In fact, many UFO researchers are beginning to ignore "lights in the sky" reports because they are almost certainly atmospheric **phenomena**.

Some perfectly natural clouds look amazingly like UFOs.

Cloud shapes

How many times have you seen clouds that look like people's faces or animals? Clouds can also be mistaken for flying saucers, especially a type called lenticular clouds. Lenticular clouds are formed when wind blows over mountain tops and is made to flow up and down like a wave. As the air rises, saucer-shaped clouds are formed.

Stranger still are noctilucent clouds. These are very high-**altitude** clouds. They form ten times higher, 48 miles (80 kilometers), than normal clouds and are made up of ice particles. After sunset, the sun's rays hit them in such a way that they look like glowing purple spaceships.

20

Mirages

A **mirage** is an image of an object that is not really there. People have even seen mirages of cities appear in the sky across seas or oceans. Mirages are caused by changes in the temperature in different layers of air. Light rays coming from objects can be bent up or down as they pass through the layers of air. On a hot summer day, have you ever seen a "puddle" on the road that disappeared as you neared it? What you actually saw is a mirage of the sky.

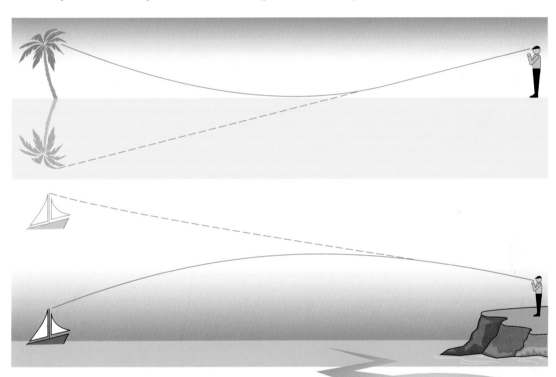

In these diagrams, the dotted lines show where the light appears to come from because of the mirage effect.

Sun and moon dogs

Under certain atmospheric conditions, rays of light from the sun or moon are bent inside clouds. When this happens, two more suns or moons appear at either side of the real one. The lights hover in the sky. These optical illusions are called "sun" or "moon dogs."

Lights or Lightning?

Lightening is often mistaken for "spaceship lights." Lightning is caused by **static electricity** that builds up in clouds and is released to the ground. A huge electric current passes through the air, creating a sparklike glow. Sheet lightning causes the whole sky to light up. It is sometimes reported to be the flash of spaceship engines.

Balls of light and fireballs

One of the strangest and spookiest of all weather **phenomena** is called ball lightning. It usually occurs just after a thunderstorm. It looks like a glowing ball of light and is about the size of a football. Eyewitnesses have reported to have seen ball lightning under the control of an "intelligent" force. The force directs it to float through their houses, follow their cars, drift through their aircraft, and even shoot up into the air. It is no wonder that people connect ball lightning to UFOs. Scientists do not yet understand how ball lightning forms or travels. However, they do know that it is an electrical phenomenon because engineers working on power lines have occasionally seen ball lightning form during their work.

A fireball is another phenomenon that occasionally happens during thunderstorms. A fireball is a huge glowing ball that seems to drop from the sky. Because it is mainly gas, it sets fire to anything it touches and can explode violently. It also interferes with electrical equipment. Fireballs are not fully understood. Scientists think they may be a special form of ball lightning. Could ball lightning be the cause of reports of spaceships crashing to Earth?

Glowing vortices

British tornado and whirlwind expert Dr. Terence Meaden believes that many UFO reports are linked to another mystery —the formation of crop circles. These circular patterns mysteriously appear in crop fields. Dr. Meaden's Plasma Vortex Theory suggests that spinning, glowing bodies of electrically charged air create crop circles. They move in a similar "intelligent" way to ball lightning. They also create *humming* sounds. Could these appear to be UFOs?

Many believe that crop circles are messages left by aliens. Dr. Terence Meaden believes that both phenomena can be explained by his Plasma Vortex Theory.

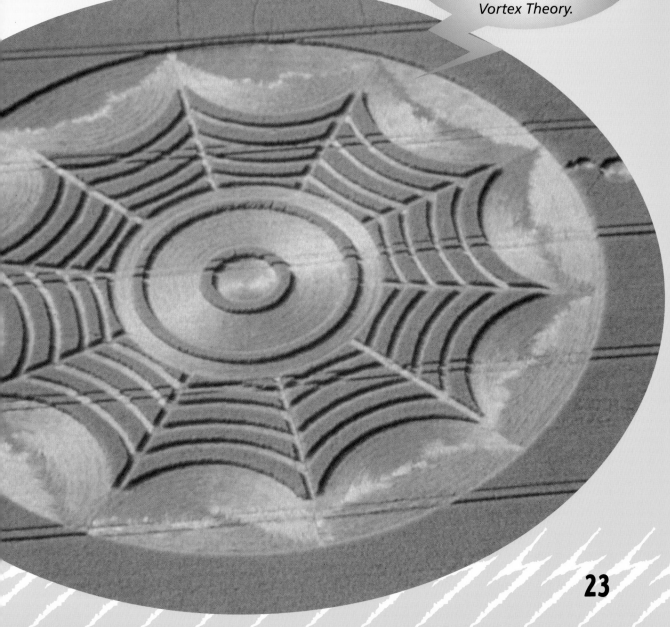

Famous Fakes

Often mysterious happenings and events that draw a lot of attention turn out to be clever hoaxes. As you might suspect, there are plenty of UFO hoaxes. Hoaxes create doubt and make all UFO reports look foolish. There are two types of UFO hoaxes: reports of sightings or abductions and fake photographs. Although not all reports are true, not all false claims are fakes. Some people may be reporting dreams that they remember as and think are real events.

Group of UFOs, Sheffield, 1962

In 1962, two schoolboys from Sheffield, England, claimed they had a photograph of a formation of five UFOs flying over Sheffield. The newspapers printed it, calling it the "best UFO photograph ever." UFOlogists exhibited it as proof of an alien visit. Ten years later, one of the boys admitted that the photograph was a fake. He said that they had painted five saucer shapes on a sheet of glass and taken a photograph through it. Even after his confession, believers in UFOs were reluctant to believe that the photograph was a hoax.

Many people thought this 1962 photograph captured UFOs over Yorkshire, England. It is a fake.

This is the famous Mexico City photograph, suspected to be an elaborate fake.

Fake aliens

There are not only fake photographs of UFOs, but also of aliens. One of the most famous is of an alien who is said to have survived a spaceship crash near Mexico City in the 1950s. The photograph is suspected of being a fake because it is out of focus and no trace has been found of the alien's body or its spacecraft.

Spotting the fake

*Some UFO photographs are obvious fakes, but some are more difficult to spot. Photographic experts are usually able to tell whether a photograph has been "doctored" after it has been taken by looking at the film's grain under a microscope. Two things to look for in a fake photograph are the difference in detail between the landscape and the UFO, and whether the UFO is blurred—this often suggests it is a model. Modern **digital photography** and computer photo-editing will make fakes easier to do and more difficult to spot.*

Why Fake UFOs?

No one doubts that there are many made-up stories of UFOs and plenty of fake photos of alien spacecraft. But why do people go to the trouble of making up stories and faking photographs? Perhaps the Sheffield schoolboys or those who created the Mexico City photograph did it for fun, attention, or to experiment with a camera. Others may do it in hopes of making money.

Selling your story

Is there money to be made by creating a UFO hoax? The story must be original, well written, and convincing enough to sell. Some national newspapers and magazines would need to investigate the story before they bought it. In the 1950s, it was easier to sell this type of story. Today, one would be competing with the thousands of reports of UFOs and alien abductions made every year. Would a good photo of a flying saucer or alien do the trick? With **digital photography** and computer graphics, it would be investigated very closely. Not every article, picture, or book on the subject is meant to fool the public. Some UFOlogists have written books on the subject.

The magazine Fate *may be delighted to have an "exclusive" alien story.*

Is it all a hoax?

Some people argue that all claims of UFO sightings and alien **abductions** are made up. They believe that all photographs of **extraterrestrials** are fakes. It is true that hoaxes are being exposed all the time. But it is also true that some reports of UFOs are made by reliable witnesses. Do you think UFOs are all a hoax, or might some be real?

How to fake a UFO picture

You could try faking your own flying saucer photograph. Throw saucer-shaped objects into the air in front of the camera, take photographs through a window in which there is a reflection of a light, or through a window with spaceships taped to it. You could try scanning photographs into a computer.

Creating UFO pictures is easy with a computer. It is harder to convince people today because they are used to seeing ads like this.

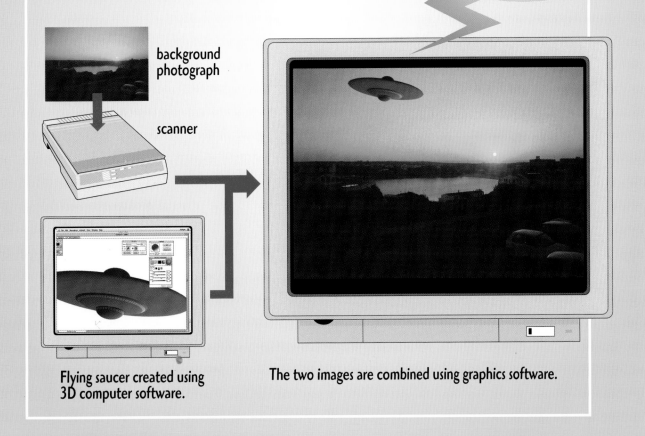

background photograph

scanner

Flying saucer created using 3D computer software.

The two images are combined using graphics software.

In Conclusion

Can science really solve the mystery of UFOs? It's certain that science, especially **meteorology**, can explain many UFO sitings. In the future, when we better understand electrical effects in the atmosphere, such as ball lightning, it may be possible to explain many more. But at the moment, there are still many UFOs that science cannot explain.

Many scientists dismiss eyewitness reports as the ramblings of attention-seekers. But what science cannot prove is that all these reports are false. Some of the reports come from reliable witnesses, such as pilots and military workers. Some UFOs are seen by groups of people in the same place at the same time. Supporters of the alien theory have no conclusive proof that **extraterrestrials** are visiting the earth. But neither do the people who don't believe in UFOs.

There is no doubt that there are UFOs. But are they from other planets? With the help of science we are beginning to find other planets in the universe. We don't have the technology to reach them to find out—not yet.

This picture shows a UFO over Charlotte, North Carolina, in 1971.

Does this photo show aliens about to invade or a flash of lightning over Sao Paulo, Brazil, in 1984.

What do you think?

Now you have read about UFOs and some possible explanations for them. Can you draw your own conclusions? Do you think that you can dismiss any of the theories without investigating them further? Do you believe that there could be life on other planets? Do you have any theories of your own?

Can we accept eyewitness accounts? What about those that tell of meetings with aliens and **abductions?** Are you disbelieving of the alien theory because of some wild claims by people? Think about whether aliens could be visiting us. If they are, what might they be looking for? Why hasn't everyone seen them?

Keep an open mind. If scientists throughout history had not investigated everything, no matter how strange or mysterious it seemed, many scientific discoveries may never have been made.

29

Glossary

abduction kidnapping

altitude height of an object above the earth's surface

astronomer scientist who studies space and the objects in space

binary computer code made up of the digits 1 and 0, which act as "on" and "off" signals

Cold War time period from 1945, just after World War Two, to about 1990, when there was a political struggle between the United States and countries of Western Europe on one side and the Soviet Union and countries of Eastern Europe on the other side

conspiracy theory idea that says that a group of people have plotted together to keep information from the public

constellation group of stars that form a pattern when they are seen from the earth

digital photography photography using computer memory chips instead of film

extraterrestrial object or lifeform that does not come from Earth

fossil remains of an ancient animal or plant

galaxy huge group of stars in space that contain billions of stars

hallucination sights, sounds, or events that appear real but are not

meteoroid piece of rock, dust, or ice from space that falls into the earth's atmosphere

meteorology science that studies the earth's atmosphere and what causes the weather

mirage image of an object in the air or water that is not really there, caused by light being bent through layers of air in the atmosphere

30

NASA (National Aeronautics and Space Administration) the organization that overseas the US space program

optical illusion vision or image that tricks the eye into seeing something that is not there

orbit path an object, such as a moon or a satellite, takes as it moves around a star or a planet

phenomenon remarkable or unexplained happening

radar device used to locate objects and determine their size and the speed in which they are moving

satellite object that moves around a star, planet, or moon in an orbit

solar system sun and its family of planets and moons

static electricity electricity that builds up on objects that are rubbed together

More Books to Read

Herbst, Judith. *The Mystery of UFOs.* Old Tappan, NJ: Simon & Schuster Children's, 1997.

Innes, Brian. *The Mysteries of UFOs.* Austin, Tex: Raintree Steck-Vaughn, 1999.

Landau, Elaine. *UFOs.* Brookfield, Conn: Millbrook Press, 1995.

Wilson, Colin (ed.). *UFOs & Aliens.* New York: DK Publishing, 1997.

Index